Sliced Tongue & Pearl Cufflinks

Kittie Belltree was born in south London. Her poems and short stories have been published in a range of journals and anthologies including *Orbis*, *The North*, *Under the Radar*, *I am not a silent poet*, *Poetry Wales*, *New Welsh Review*, *The Lampeter Review* and *Brittle Star*. A pamphlet of her poems, *moon in scorpio*, was shortlisted for the Venture Award 2015 and she then received a Literature Wales Mentoring Bursary to develop this into a first full collection. Kittie has been highly commended in the Welsh International Poetry Competition, the Penfro Poetry Festival Competition, The Camden and Lumen Poetry Competition and the Orbis Readers Award. She works as a Specialist Tutor for students with neurodiversities and learning differences at Aberystwyth University where she is also completing a part-time PhD. Off campus she teaches creative writing in the community where she has worked with home-educated teenagers and people with dementia. Kittie lives in a tiny cottage overlooking the Teifi Estuary that she shares with her partner, daughter and an unspecified number of felines.

Sliced Tongue & Pearl Cufflinks

Kittie Belltree

Dear Chloe,

I hope you enjoy the poems, warm wishes

Kittie Belltree

oct '2014

S.

PARTHIAN

Parthian, Cardigan SA43 1ED www.parthianbooks.com
First published in 2019
© Kittie Belltree 2019
ISBN 978-1-912681-14-3
Editor: Susie Wild
Cover Image by Lianette Art and Design
Cover design by Emily Courdelle
Author photo by Marc Hayes Photography
Typeset by Elaine Sharples
Printed and bound by 4edge Limited, UK
Published with the financial support of the Books Council of Wales
British Library Cataloguing in Publication Data
A cataloguing record for this book is available from the British Library.

'… *For years I put off telling the tale of my voyage to W.'*
– Georges Perec, *W or The Memory of Childhood*

Contents

IV. The Whole Thing Looks like it Could Collapse at Any Moment

I.

Unspoken

A short poem about my mother, who could hear a pin drop on a motorway

I'm trying to write a poem.
It's about my mother.
When I finish it, it will be so deep, so dark and dislocating
spilling all the years of suffering so eloquently
with a voice so suffused in beauty and truth
that she would put down her
gardening gloves, or paring knife, or knitting needles
and her heart would break. Instantly.

My words alone would make her
look over her life with fresh eyes, filled
with such sorrow, she would despise
herself for turning her back
on the one good thing she never had.
Or, it would strike her down dead, even –
this poem I'm going to write.
Even though she will never see it – still
I keep trying to write this poem about my mother.

Only when I write this poem
will I be able to write
all the other poems I have stagnating inside.
Why, there's a whole stack.
Keeping mum. Holding back.
It's just this poem about my mother I keep trying to write.

I've tried beating it out of me
starving it, stuffing it
yelling, screaming, taking away its favourite things
like shopping trips
chocolate and lazy nights in with a *film noir* and a slim gin.
But still, it won't spill.
Still, I'm working on this poem about my mother.

I've been working on this poem (on and off)
since I started writing poetry.
It's undergone many drafts over the years.
Once, in a dream, I finished writing this poem about my mother.
Then, in the yawn of morning
I stuffed those pages somewhere I can't find.
Though I know they exist.
That's why I keep trying to write this poem about my mother.

I keep getting stuck on this one line.
I think it's a good line, with a quietly restrained half-rhyme.
I know she'll never see it, but
I want to follow it with something
so touching, so tender, it would render
her speechless. And she would immediately be
cleansed of all cynicism, resentment

and other animosities that leave
a bitter twist on the tongue, get on a train
and come show me her wounds.
And it would be a miracle.

Perhaps I should leave it out, but the poem
I'm trying to write
seems to want this one line.
Peace comes when the hate is gone.
Is that something she should know?
I think it's from Thelonious Monk singing 'Five Spot Blues'.
Perhaps I wish she listened to the blues
instead of Beethoven, Bach or Bruch.
Or just listened even.

      I keep trying to write this poem about my mother.
      I want it to be something beautiful, something other.
      Something all those who have ever felt
      the ravening reflex of loving hands
      or knuckles, or broomsticks
      or dressing-gown chords
      will resonate with.
      Even though no one will ever see it.

I keep trying to write this poem about my mother.
I want it to be perfect.
I want it to contain the word *superciliousness.*
I'm just needing to draw this line.
I'm just waiting to hear it.

Descent

It was the eleventh hour of the eleventh day of the eleventh month. We were outside the Co-op in the rain on the parade, where you rattled hearts for change with your red collecting box. (We'd been there every weekend since the spiders came in from the woods.) It was still streaming knives and forks when we got the bus back home and after supper, I stayed up and watched *The Festival of Remembrance* on T.V. How the poppies tumbled in a titanic hush like squillions of silent sycamore seeds. It was black and white. But inside my head the poppies fell in colour. Later, I noticed that some had fallen in our back garden. They grew into the kind of deep, dark forest you find in fairy tales. I remember, because I was eleven eleven eleven.

My Father's City

To visit you, these days I wear the bridle and the bit.
You could make an exhibit of my tongue
place it alongside the crystal skull
or the torture chair in the Horniman Museum.

I had nightmares after your wife took me there.
And mumps. My throat puffed
like the stuffed walrus, and I could not speak
for weeks.   Afterwards, I dreamed

you were an anteater – when I felt the deep
strokes of your long, safe tongue I knew
I could make a stable of my body for generations
of War and Hate. To celebrate, we rode

on silver double-decker buses with blood-
red carpets in the aisles, and you promised me a pony
ride at Crystal Palace Zoo.   In the newspapers
it was there in black and white

but all the queen's horses and all the queen's men
wore such fine colours, it was easier to pretend
to be asleep. When I awoke, your gates were closed
and an iron bar blistered my palate.

It's been thirty winters since you showed me
how empty a city can be.   At weekends
you took me to football, wrapped me round your neck
to keep the chill from your pharynx.

Portrait of the Family after the War

For me, the world as I knew it and the people in it emerged not from the
womb, but from war

– Eva Hoffman

And if you saw it – propped between carved wooden clock
and chipped china doves, perched on the over-mantel
above the old gas fire; fogged with dust – it was just in passing.

For there was much dust then, between them and us.
It gusted like bankruptcy from an un-named state
and you were benumbed by stiff brushes and godliness.

Perhaps the photographer's young assistant
unseen in half-lit backroom behind velvet drapes
touching-up phantasmagorias from trays of transparent tints

or some lingering studio apparition; a departed sweetheart
heaving body and tongue from hot tungsten, caught the moment
Father braced shoulders back, Mother reached hands

to settle restless children before the shutter
sealed, in wordless black and white, the instant the light exposed
the place they'd dreamed of calling home was nowhere.

Nachträglich

(afterwards)

only the clock
on the mantelpiece
could speak

while all the hours
of my life
fell silent

afraid of wanting
and being found
wanting

Photograph Albums of the Dead

Thick pages separated with tissue
embossed, yellowing sticky
corner pieces, wings of dead flies.
Always a child in a sailor suit,
a stroll on the prom, a great rick
of a harvest; sleeves rolled, hands
on. Time turning over – a wedding

with a cake made of industrial
promises and Polyfilla. A dress
stitched specially for the occasion
from a tablecloth and net curtains
by a woman who never spoke
with a spit-soaked needle
and an eye that pierces stone.

Then the missing ones – black
holes bordered by the bleach of time
that snitch and snatch like nursery rhymes.
And always this darkness:
it lived at the top of the stairs
in the house where you were born.

Unspoken I

after Owen Sheers

It was a school photo – taken in '78
the too-blue skyscape
still swirled in the background

while the corners slipped
under slender half-moon slits
in the fuzzled cardboard frame.

I'm wearing washed-out PE kit
squashed beside my pig-tailed
big sister with her head-girl eyes.

She's in her textbook-black
serge blazer; brilliant
with badges for every school prize.

I knew my grandmother
would get it for Christmas
picture-perfect, tucked inside

a newsy letter stuffed
with snatches and slices of life
snippets from *Family Circle* recipes and lies.

I'd wanted to sharpen the focus
put her in the picture.
So I messed up my uniform

lost my tie, mimed words
my cast-off mouth could not disguise,
turned down like an invitation.

She never replied
until I found this photograph
waiting among her dead things,

then your face flashed at me

though you were not yet my child.

The Magician's Daughter

In the fairy stories, the daughters love their fathers because they are mighty princes,
great rulers, and because such absolute power seduces.
— Carolyn Steedman, *Landscape for a Good Woman*

He draws a silk scarf from a secret pocket in his trousers – snakes
it around wrists, splits in two, twists it taut, like her vocal cords,
places it over her eggshell eyelids, then offers his hand – white-gloved
bowing low, he lets loose the stolen jewels lining his jacket.

She accepts – blindly – curtseying into the citrine shaft
of spotlight that slices the stage in half, then footsteps
into the dead-flat chest, arranges herself – doll-like – inside
before he lays the wooden lid to rest.

Until now he has kept her for himself, fed on a diet of sliced
tongue and pearl cufflinks. The ritual begins before the stage
door, before the audience, the dressing room – where he inserts
the knife into her velvet and feathers, plucks

her hair into tucks and tresses, places a glass
slipper on her pillow. Thus he enters without breaking
and she slips seamlessly into the space conjured by his third wife
who broke all his spells while he snored by the stove

after Saturday *matinée*, stole the key to his best hat-box
for her whale-bone combs and peacock frocks,
and vanished with a ventriloquist from Vladivostok.
He feels the thickness of the blade like honey inside her

and the strength of his heaving old magic. Why, his wand
can cut her in two – separate her bones from her meat
like halving a peach. She is ripe, now, for his next trick –
Now he has her undone, he will make her disappear. Now –

It was the same thing every Christmas

Lying in a crumpled heap on the floor
Say thank you again and again
I must not forget
Folds in half and in half again

Say thank you again and again
Mother presses out the creases
Folds in half and in half again
Repeating itself in my head

Mother presses out the creases
Now I send them to my nieces
Repeating itself in my head
The word ungrateful

Now I send them to my nieces
I must not forget
The word ungrateful
Lying in a crumpled heap on the floor

Separated at Birth

By accident we found ourselves
on opposite sides   so I turned
myself into a paper bag to survive

the war. After all   what can a paper
bag say   or do   but carry your many
secrets and your outright lies

and remain hidden – a perfect
disguise. When I thought
it was safe   I revealed myself

but you accused me of having
an easy ride. But here are your
secrets and your lies   I kept them

for you I cried. I slipped under
doors   I folded myself into the size
of a cigarette paper   what more could I do?

In the distance   a street light flickered
and a bell rang three times   before you
crumpled me into nothing in your empty hands.

Psylocybin and the Psymptoms of Psychosis

I.

How come, when I was a kid
we were always having power cuts?

Once, I remember

we were sitting on the sofa in the dark
apart
from dad who was lying
down in the hall
his head inside the cupboard-
under-the-stairs, looking for candles.
How come the orange hum
of street lights never went on power cuts?
How come they always happened
When *The Generation Game* was on?
Pyyyummmmmm and the lights went and the picture
shrunk
a dot of white light
staying for a minute or two, then
gone?

II.

Don't look now, but that woman over there. She keeps staring at me. I told
you not to look. The one sitting over there. Next to the woman who's
wearing the same top as you. *What woman?*

III.

How come drinking

mushroom tea
on a ferry 'cross the Irish Sea; don't
pretend you don't know what I'm talking about

16

when I say I was on a section three.
I must confess you know my life's a mess
that's right some days I don't –
feel-like-cleaning their signs
of neglect and that bargain
bin pathology – if you buy
me you get me
free?

IV.

My mother, Erika, was shouting at
my dad, George, that he had the wrong
colour
candles. Not to burn the red
ones because she was saving them for Christmas.

V.

I saw her again on the tube. She was sitting opposite me, reading some trashy
chick-lit. She kept crossing and uncrossing her legs and I could see sweat
sticking in the folds of skin behind her knees. That skirt is way too short.
She's been shopping for clothes. *NEW LOOK.* The carrier bag sagged at her
feet gives her away. I'd never buy clothes from there. I'm forty-nine for
Christ sakes.

VI.

Dad is lying
down in the hall.
He has broken
the mirror
that hung next to the clothes-brush
He is picking-up
the bits and pieces of broken
faces
and hands being careful
not to cut
fingers.

How come the mirror broke?
I ask. Don't Tell
Your Mother, he answers

VII.
How come hearing
visions seeing voices
clear as a bell through the fog
of Fishguard Harbour 2am
thought-I'd sleep-on-the-train
automatic doors keep me from
falling
awake after a cup
of Great Western
Gnat's Piss
doing the cross-
word phat-
phingered newspaper
pholded in halph
and then
in halph again?

VIII.
My dad was lying down again in the hall
with his head inside the cupboard-under-
the-stairs. He emptied the contents
of the meter into his palm and held up a coin.
This one was unusually shiny and new-looking.
He rolled it across his knuckles
flicked it in the air, then caught it against
the back of his hand.
Heads or tails? He winked.

IX.

I mean jeans are one thing. Jeans are fine. I live in jeans. But these weren't jeans. Jeans are supposed to be comfortable. These were cut so low you wouldn't be able to sit down in them without revealing half your arse. And the top – so flimsy you could look through it.
I tried them on. Later. When the girls were playing and I heard the *bleep-bubble-bleep* of *Supermario* collecting coins. I tried them on. *Mamamia-bubble-bleep.* They fitted. *That Princess is a Peach bleep-bleep.* I clocked my rear view in the full-length mirror. Just as I thought. Who does she think she is? She's a shopaholic and an alcoholic and a workaholic too. She is. *Bleep.*

X.

How come the sensation
the self-attribution
broken
replaced
by a name sewn into a neck
displaced
by a zebra crossing
the road
to the self
is closed
while I stand on the other side
of mind watching
television with the light
out in a house filled with rooms
I dare not inhabit
a tiny dot appears
on the screen I dare not enter
the whites of your eyes circling the perimeter
twisting
me
into bits
or is it pieces
the two of me

fitting
perfect
enigma?

XI.
Tails, I answered.
He peaked at the coin under his palm,
tossed it back up into the air, caught it, then put it in his pocket with the rest.

My Milk Chocolate Grandmother

My milk chocolate Grandmother
My *Kinder Surprise* Grandmother
My *eins zwei drei* Grandmother

My *guten Morgen* Grandmother
My Luton airport Grandmother
My I couldn't explain, even to myself Grandmother

My *Dumkopf* Grandmother
My pfifty *pfenig* Grandmother
My *Fröhliche Weihnachten* Grandmother

My memory moves inside me Grandmother
My *ich liebe dich* Grandmother
My like a second heart Grandmother

My *Kasper singt la la la* Grandmother
My try to remember the words Grandmother
My *der Teufel singt lo lo lo* Grandmother

My as if we could ever forget Grandmother
My *Heil Hitler* Grandmother
My *du bist ein böses Kind* Grandmother

My goes without saying Grandmother

Poem for a sister

Did I never tell
the story of how I lost   my i
in a bed of broken glass

watching soot black tears
slip   into the body of silence
that lies in the gap   between

the platform and the train?
How I couldn't say   mother
because I had let that   word   go.

Unspoken II

A secret fell from a seventh floor window – flung out in a frenzied exchange. As it plummeted, incidents from its life raced across the face of the moon. The secret saw its birth – small, insignificant, why – so small, it spent its first few years in a pocket. Then there was shouting; being hurled at a door, followed by a shoe, then a bottle or two. Being stamped on, stretched and twisted, hidden in the back of a drawer. It remembered a warm welcome, the ache of a young woman's heart. The brittle mystery of wintering there, before landing on its pants in the street. Good times, bad times, being woken at dawn, dragged out, slapped – still it lived on – voiceless, true to its word, spending these last few years folded between pages of *The Complete Works of Oscar Wilde*. The secret, having held its tongue against the decades, decades of late nights and insults, cried out at the cruel stab of the jabbering river. But the moon shrank from the shriek of silence, the spell broke, the secret sank and the river licked its heart – its tears drowned by the sound of the watercourse, its soul aground against the bitter grit of the river's crooked-sixpence bed. Later, a woman with no hair and a long name that everyone had forgotten, noticed its remains by the Strand where, last summer, a child was found with its hand on the shore. The woman wept so openly – having no secrets of her own to hold, I was moved to give her mine.

II.

So Much Blood

Loose Lips Sink Ships

I

Don't you know there's a war on?

she was upstairs playing dolls
in the box room
when fingers snatched handfuls of hair

parsimoniously they plucked
the raw chords still in her throat
while she played

dead to the thud of her head
on the floorboards
and the rasp of sheets torn into bandages

II

Hold your tongue.

there was no blood
only the stump
of her to slump into a shroud

and a few silly tears to wipe
from eyelids that rattled
in a brittle oversized head

and closed when she lay down
as though she had
been put to death

III
She never spoke about her family.

when mother hoisted *her* head high
the small square of silence
swelled in the hollow of her mouth

They drowned she said to the sea
in her head
while a troop of tin soldiers

filed into the box room
to fill the space with nothing
and no body to speak of

W or The Death of Me

This morning, when I opened my mouth a black dog sprang out. Followed by a whole pack. Howling out of my mouth. Next came strangers in serge suits smelling of mothballs with eyes like market fish. A slow succession of hearses. An entire funeral procession. Long, drawn-out. Years of yowling, bestial grief. When I opened my mouth. There was no place for this mourning in the narrow streets outside my house, so I nodded at the neighbours, pulled my lips into line, hoped the corners wouldn't crack; spill hordes of wailing women, one-by-one out of my mouth, so what starts as just a gentle hum becomes a roar louder than a jet engine, spewing bitter black smoke. Out of my mouth. She wanted all of it. Me. The house. All the furniture. The car, too. All of it. This morning, I heaved an oil slick of sorrow. I swirled about in it. I drowned in it. Feeling the stick in her throat, finding my way in the cellar of her gut where earthworms spiralled from the bloody walls and words became dust. This mourning, when I opened my mouth, I swallowed hard as her fingers dug me up, as she twisted my tongue into a double helix and ate it. Out of my mouth. My mother. For her own story.

After the *Führer*

Women's hearts are like battles. They are not won through hesitation
– Adolf Hitler

Don't stop my mother as she rocks
around the clock in sky-blue satin
twirling wordless renunciation
like a stainless knife.

Don't speak when she sways
her hush-hush hips at American soldiers
who vow they'll show her how
to Jitterbug, Jump and Jive.

Don't ask for a taste of the man
to share his sweetness before he crumbles
as *mutti* presses shapes from dough
gingerbread men for the oven.

Don't pry into why she left
the motherland as if white cliffs
might ward off
any sense of being

implicated, connected to me.
Don't mention the absurdity,
the mere suggestion,
that in England

with papers and scissors
her attachment
to the man himself
would just disappear from memory.

Heirloom Recipe

in the kitchen
a stranger with my mother's eyes
says

          i sift between scales
          i strain
          the method

i'll lose you on purpose
get you lost
in these dark woods

          of memory – girl
          thing, and then girl again –
          a liquid

she was wearing an apron
kneading a yeasty
dough

          eye – a sleep, a slit
          where mother's love lies
          in the pantry, in her pocket

dusty specks of flour
crumble in the cracks of her knuckles
where the spiders crawl

          unanswered
          each waking – a going-under
          what does the body know

at night, they spin and stitch
while she whips me
in the cold-room

          forgetting
          is the secret ingredient
          peel, pare, poke, poach

my mouth
a gash in the burlap
of her apron

          a measure of eye
          a lid to tighten silence
          prepare a whole from its holes

Don't mention it

Speaking is silver, silence is gold
– German Proverb

A new kitchen and a Kenwood Chef don't make
it better I'm from London England and you're
not but that don't matter any longer not
to me you in your fuming mad coat
stamping and marching us and them
and up and down them god-damned stairs
and what did *we* know about what it was like for you.

Dirty dirty everything was dirty just like you
always said it was filth fouling out of every brick
and orifice every glass every bone every crack.
And I have to agree filthy fucking me scoured
knees and under my chewed and spat out
nails and all that Englishness to scrub
and pick away at till it was sore. Brat.

It was just like you said it was you
belonged some place else without all that
soot from the *Parkray* rain and them squat
squalid kids needing to be washed without
waiting for buses without meat and two veg
noisy nosy neighbours *Pick of the Pops* without

me. Like I said it don't matter. You were
just keeping mum leaving layers of memory
squished into a Clark's shoebox under the bed
where you said it belonged shut up about all them
dead men at the end of the pendulum who
never swung home again when the clock struck ten
you were angry like clockwork and I was a mouse
child ticking inside still you've not showed me

his picture never said his name once the third
time I asked you to love me like the motherland
flames flared from your nostrils scorched the walls
of our house you made me get down on my knees
and scrape it off but that don't matter. It was
sloppy of me another slip up and beg what
happened to fascists after the war did they stop

being fascists and take up a hobby do crosswords
or did they not it don't matter anymore because
they are former and we are informed uniformed
like terraced houses closed doors shut down
shut up shops that sell everything cheaper for
the price of silence soon every home will have
one and another free junk food for thought I'd say

sorry thought I'd say it don't matter you know
I know you were just following orders un-doing
the past like you were told three times before
the cock crows and I don't even know him
in the story about the family after the war
where the war is the eye and the heart
and the tongue there's no need to speak about the un-

Germans the truth lies in the actions the rubble
the bridges burned that was the day you stamped
your foot through the floorboards and made Daddy's
Girl come out from the fault in the wood the slip
up and I don't blame you she was born this way
and assumes full responsibility for all your pain.

London is so dirty these days rowdy streets rattling
with unclean kids you were in the dining room
listening to Beethoven's 5th Bach's suite No.3
in D minor Schumann's *Traumerie* my throat
changed shape trying to get my blunt English
tongue to swallow the German word for dream.

What the magpie told my mother

I

Your daughter will be a scapegoat.
She will know sorrow intimately,
sleep naked in doorways, crawl under fences
carrying your old linen in a suitcase

tied with a rope braided from her hair,
and a cenotaph on her back.
Even her sisters will pinch the skin
over their knuckles and call her a thief.

II

For her tenth birthday, you will give her
to a soldier for a loaf of bread
and teach her to keep a secret.
When she is hungry

you will spit over your left shoulder
chop up slivers of her tongue
bake them in a pie and make
her sing for her supper.

III

When the memories come
tell her to walk into a mirror
and gather each shard behind a locked door
in a darkened room in a house made of shoes.

I will bring a tiding of perfect black
beaks, to pluck crushed berries from her heart
show her how to liberate gold rings
have the last laugh.

My Mother's Hands

For her fingers were fillets of salt fish
her fingernails, the teeth of smothered babies
and the whorls of her fingertips, blunted mill saws
strangled with barbed wire.

For her palms were quick-setting cement
with fleshy mounds of tender *Gelignite.*
For the crease of her Lifeline was The Lost City of Atlantis
For her Headline was yesterday
and her Heartline marked a gravel path to Beachy Head.

For her joints were rows of crooked gibbets
dressed with the flesh of rotting corpses, her ligaments – *rigor mortis.*
For her wrists were pillars of salt,
her thumbs, Hitler and Mussolini
and her fists formed perfect punctuation marks for winning arguments

For the spaces between her fingers
were the telephone numbers of all the men who never called.
For they were soft as mustard gas.
For they were hard as my luck.

For they were both left and right and had a mind of their own.
For they belonged to someone else.
For they spoke a secret language.
For they were tools for telling the time
and not telling.

My Mother's Garden

I still remember the last time I tried
to tear down the tangled forest
that had eaten the path to your house.
All morning, I walked through the rain
calling your name into the mouth
of a manic storm as I hacked
at thickets with the backs of my hands.
Late afternoon, lacerated, I still remember
how I lost my shoe as I cut a throat
through your twisted clutch of thorns.
I caught the washing line – where you hung
our insides out to dry and I learned
to walk – still taut six feet above ground.
Darkness settled over trees like a flock
of birds and I still remember when
my heart was an orchard and one year
in place of apple trees, you planted fear
and told me to water it with tears
ripen it with blood, that the little black
berries were the bread of life. Each night,
after rations, I heard the moon

drop into your pond like a stone
when I swallowed my hunger for you.

So much blood

The last time we saw you was in the hospital
on a section three. You lied to the nurses
but were so convincing, one of them played
mother and poured our tea, while another
mopped up spilt milk from the tray.
When we stop and think – it does sound dumb –
really, why would you come when
you have the whole world to see?

It was an accident. We were at a crossroads.
We should have looked.
Longer. Harder. We always felt you were
just around the corner, in the next street
like neighbours who never speak. For years
we thought someone had taken you – hidden
you under a stone, or a bridge, or a tree.

When we played mother, we held on until
we heard ringing our ears – anything to smother
the silence. Call it fate – the sun was in our eyes
that morning, driving home   the empty road
the collision of our common calling.

III.

Bond

Everyone said it wouldn't last

Before it happened, I was just
a victim of highway hypnosis. Absent-
mindedly mouthing the lyrics to some September
love song, when November, with its body of bereavement
and betrayal, leapt into the headlights like a crime photograph.

I remember the radio –
how it fizzed and died alongside
The Six o clock News, and how hard
I tried to hang on to the maps, as my brake-foot broke
through the foot-well, when your words drove a hole in the world.

It was a Friday.
I'd bought bubble bath
and a bottle of red to go with the steaks.
Two days later they lie – severed from their intended parts –
seeping blood into the salad drawer. Safely removed, you let-go

my name like a gunshot.
I thought, she reminds me of
my mother, makes me think of suicide
bombers – the hopelessness trying to rationalise
the cut-and-run despair of it, as bodies collide like knuckles.

Afterwards, I combed
the blown-up image of the recent past
for relics I could string together to explain
the first day of the rest of life – the hush post-detonation
the ash-grey after-light haunting the hollow streets, abandoned houses.

The vacant liberation.

A river runs through me,

*the obsession with suicide is characteristic of the man who can neither live nor die,
and whose intention never swerves from this double possibility*

– Emil Cioran

crossing
through
my inner
landscape
like a pen.
  I on one side
   of this great
    divide, on the
     other, a strange
     woman lives
    in a house identical
   to mine. Every day
  she stands there
 outside her house
staring. I hoped
she might go
away one day
but, even at
night, when,
unable to
sleep, I
peep
behind
curtains
she is
standing
there still,
watching me.
Even when
sleep takes hold
and I go under
she is there on the
other side of mind
looking at me
with her yawning
  eyes crossing
   the water.
    Sometimes
    a river
    sometimes
    a stream,
   but always
   this body
    between us,
    this insistent
   A to B idea,
  nagging me
 to change
  the subject.

Every
 morning
I rush out
of my house
in the hope
that she will
 be gone. But
  even in the
  pouring rain
  she is there still
 standing outside
her house. I stand
there too, not knowing
what to do, 'til I am soaked
through, 'til my head aches
 and it feels like my thoughts
 no longer hold water. I shout
 across at her, I am losing
 my mind go away
I have lost my mind
but she does not reply
and my words flow
down the river
like a long
illegible
note
 I wrote
  to my self
  and lost
  sometime ago.
 In desperation
 I set fire to my house
 take off all my clothes
 and throw my self
into the river.
The current is strong.
It takes me all day long
 to swim to the opposite shore.
  It is nearly dark when I reach
  the riverbank. I crawl out
  exhausted, unable to speak.
 I look for the woman
 but there is no one there.
Only a different woman
standing on the other side
outside a burning house
watching – waiting
 for some thing
 to happen.

Miss Edge

She'd stepped out of a class at the arts centre.
We had to pluck someone from the clutch
of customers in the coffee bar queue, empty
their pockets, cut a slice from their life

describe what's inside. I forget who wrote
about the woman with no cash and a name
to match; who housed her in a high-rise,
gave her a love for the high life and a lover

who was a low-life with a wife about to drop;
who made her rock on the concrete ledge
above the flyover in fuck-me boots, her up-do
threatening to topple in the slip-stream

from double-deckers; who put on her killer heels,
turned up the volume, dressed her in red
and left this silence hanging between her legs
the day she went over the edge.

Bond

In 1945, August DeMont drove to the Golden Gate Bridge with his five-year-old daughter, Marilyn; told her to climb over the rail and jump. She did so without hesitation. Seconds later he dived gracefully after her. A note left in the car stated, 'I and my daughter have committed suicide.'

i

For that was the fact of the matter.
The fact of the matter in a sentence.
A punishment. The blunt force
of its grammar. Pragmatic
punctuation precise enough to slice
through time like a seam.

That night, the rain fell in short, pattering
clusters. Your clothes moaned in the closet.
A dog slipped out into the dark.
The quiet fact of the matter.
Seven words for sadness.
Words like stones.

ii

She never spoke. Someone said
the car seat was still warm when
they found the note.

The matter-of-fact fumbling
at the rubble of my heart.
A cigarette butt tossed into space.

iii

How to smother   a black
hole   revoke   the last
wordless   slam
of doors   annul
the unspoken bond

deeper   than any   drop
leaving me   done
with life.   A sentence   followed by

                 a full stop.

traffic

As harps for the winds of heaven,
My web-like cables are spun;
I offer my span for the traffic of man,
At the gate of the setting sun.

Not a month since that blonde stumbled
through the swingside doors and listed
against the bar. 'What's a nice girl
like you...' he'd chucked at her, tongue
tacky with cheap scotch. Clocked
the razor lines up her left arm.

As harps for the winds of heaven

They'd left for his after she'd got gritty
with the bartender who'd groused about
her foul mouth, called her a crazy bitch
when she'd shattered a glass, held it
up close to the skin of her throat. He'd
promised them both, 'She'll be alright now.'

My web-like cables are spun;

Listening to her piss in the bathroom
while he rolled a spliff, she'd garbled some
hippy shit about finding a gateway, crossing
a bridge, putting herself together again, he'd thought
how she's either crackbrain high or junkyard
low. No middle road. Only edges, thresholds.

I offer my span for the traffic of man

A note said she'd gone for cigarettes, a change
of clothes. That was a week ago. The bartender
mumbles, 'Sorry about your girl.' 'Sorry, didn't
you know? A kid saw her jump feet first.'
He slants his drink. Orders another, chasing
chinks in the passage of unbroken night.

At the gate of the setting sun.

:ard from Pwll Deri

Dewi Emrys 1879-1952
a thina'r meddilie sy'n dwad ichi pan foch chi'n ishte uwchben Pwllderi
and these are the thoughts that will come to you when you sit above Pwll Deri

Easy to miss footfalls
in the twists of thrift
to slip on loose stones –
purple, like the sun's blush.

I can almost make out my vantage point
where the yellow gorse
scorched every step –
each one, a journey, a small death.

The drop was delicious –
hung over the poison-bottle blue of the bay
a water-rush of clarity.
Sharp enough to kill time. Now

families from the Nappy Valley
between Wimbledon and West Dulwich
hire the hostel for weddings and New Year.
All they talk about is the view

from the dining room – breathtaking
like an asthma attack.
Each greedy mouth marks a giant grey O
for my dead body.

... suicide remains a courageous act, the clear headed act of a mathematician

– Graham Greene, *The Comedians*

Because of a shortfall in funds, the suicide prevention team at Beachy Head had to sell off their patrol cars, thermal imaging cameras and make four out of ten staff redundant. Because on the London Underground, the only suicide preventive measures are Platform Edge Doors on the Jubilee line extension. Because installing them elsewhere is seen as too expensive. Because millions are spent on terror prevention at these very same stations. Because certain parts of the NHS spend 6.6 percent of their budgets on mental health when it accounts for 23 percent of their burden. Because at Hornsey Lane Bridge, North London, the preventative measures consist of two-inch spikes and a rotating bar that even a small dog could step over. Because a net would cost Haringey Council £95,000 plus vat. Because English Heritage say it would compromise the bridge's Victorian architecture. Because after cleanup; emergency services; counselling for witnesses and families, plus tax not paid into the system, each suicide in England ends up costing £1.45 million. Because roughly 1,600 people have perished at San Francisco's Golden Gate Bridge since it opened in 1937. Because this figure only includes incidents in which a body was recovered or someone saw the jump. Because the bridge offers a near-perfect 99 percent success rate with almost every jumper exploding internally upon impact. Because about 5 percent who survive the initial force drown or die of hypothermia. Because the official count ended on June 5, 1995 with the 997th jump. Because a shock jock offered a case of *Snapple* soft drinks to the family of the 1000th suicide victim. Because the most suicides in one month occurred in August 2013, when 10 people jumped from the Bridge; one every three days. Because the 1.5 percent who do survive the plunge strike the water feet-first and at a slight angle.

IV.

The Whole Thing Looks like it Could Collapse at Any Moment

Guilty by dissociation

my
name
is a gunshot
an accusation
from this hook
some long-dead thing
swings – rotting in its knotted
clutch of consonants – a confidence
trickster shuffling in queues
my name is blood-
stained stitched
into the back
of my neck
shame
mud

Wash dark colours separately

See reverse for care instructions

I must have left a poem there when
I put down my pen to sort her drawers.

Reshape whilst damp

As if writing could make her whole
explain the past, shape the future.

Dry away from direct heat

I thought she was gone for good
'til I heard her death rattle

Do not bleach

like a belt buckle against the drum,
watched her vanish into the fog of the spin cycle.

Do not tumble dry

As if writing about her
could clear the fog
that pushes and sighs
against my pen.

As if writing about her
could move the mountain.
The stack of dishes killing time
the sheets to fold and hang.

Always read the label

My arms ache with the weight
of wet washing. There's the supper to pull
out of a hat. As if writing about her
could stop the cycle in mid rotation.

The art of moving an upright piano into an upstairs flat

In the time it takes to switch on my phone
it's already on Youtube. Mark, the JCB driver
mimics my anxious face as he climbs into his cab.
This morning he lifted a static caravan

a rust-gnawed Renault Trafic
and an old school bus before breakfast
my husband says. I'm a worrier.
I gulp as Mark nods him to slip

two flimsy-looking loops
over the front forks, felling
the neighbours' wall with just a tap
of those titanic tyres as he reverses.

Passengers from the Poppit Rocket
give up their seats as the Old Joanna puffs out
two decades of dust, quavers, creaks then she's up –
faltering at first, the way a Li-lo fills

after winter in the loft – then she wings
over the bent-back heads of eyewitnesses
aiming mobile phones, my screams swamped
by the holiday traffic honking choc-o-bloc

up and down the street as she soars –
then snags her brass bun feet in telephone wires.
I shut my eyes and try not to think
about half the village with its Broadband down

or what happens to those tacky soft toys
swung from the crooked jaws
of some sly fairground goody-grabber.
I open them as a lorry driver leaps out

shares a laugh about Laurel and Hardy with my other half
while she hangs like a coffin rocking on air
they take hold of my washing pole
and length of two-by-two.

Romeo y Julieta

A man and a woman are playing cards.
It is as it should be – in a dimly lit room
on a folding table with a green felt top.
The whole thing looks like it could collapse

at any moment. She handles the hearts
like a pro, dividing the deck with bitten
lips, long sleeves and wounded nail-polish.
He traces the presence of absence

with a fat cigar and the weight
of a single malt mixed with moonlight.
What have they got to be smiling about?
Later, on the table, matches are stacked

and pennies, and at least thirty
pieces of silver, like little leaning
towers. She wears the scent of long
dead flowers. He is afraid of heights.

On the morning of September 11, 2001

Nineteen men tooled up with Stanley knives and fronted by a man
on renal dialysis from his hillside hideout on the other
side of the freedom-loving peace-keeping Western world
carried out the most sophisticated security breach in history –
penetrating ultra-protected airspace while staying hidden –
using only a laptop and mobile phones. This man under question

despite all the cutting-edge tech we're told not to question
evaded detection for a decade and made thirty-five videos of a man
who defied the laws of time. Perhaps because he stayed hidden
so long, dodging skin damage from the desert sun. On the other
hand, some say he lived on the run and if you followed the story
he always escaped – despite the military might of the world's

most powerful nation in chase. Before holding the world
to ransom, the nineteen devoutly religious men in question
were spotted downing beers, snorting coke and, so the story
goes, hanging out with strippers. One emailed his German
mate with intimate details of the attack date, while another
had flying lessons and hired a 'plane but kept his ID hidden

from authorities and instructors, who stated in no hidden
terms that he couldn't fly a *Cessna* and was the world's
worst pilot. Still, he executed a corkscrew turn (as the others
overpowered passengers and crew on four full flights); questioning
the laws of physics and evading radar for hours. The men
then took out three buildings with two 'planes (a first in aviation history)

descending 8000 feet at 270 degrees, striking the first storey
of the Pentagon finance office – bullseye (where news of a hidden
or missing $2.3 trillion was announced by a budget analysis man
only the day before at a press conference in front of the world).
But the pundits and politicians didn't have to ask questions;
they knew all about the men within minutes of each other

because they saw all the hallmarks plus one or the other's
passport fell from the sky and miraculously survived the hysteria.
Some folks in tinfoil hats began asking awkward questions
about Building 7, dustification, Flight 93, the BBC, hidden
drills with hijacked aircraft being flown into buildings, The World
Trade Centre lease and trillion dollar insurance scams. Kinsmen

if you question this story or raise any other doubts about hidden
agendas, secret weapons, psyops, false flags, or the new world
order you're a paranoid conspiracy theorist, a traitor – inhuman.

On paper

I

Isn't that just what one does while the clock is ticking, the tap is dripping
the bombs exploding on the other side of the fence? One plays the role.
One is born one lives one dies; another one afraid to tell the story of ones' selves.

II

How else to survive the poison pressing the psyche like a doorbell?
How else to snooze amidst the incessant sound of human heartbreak
unaware that this is the situation in the daily administration?

III

There is always an other thing to do between tea breaks and traffic
lights.   It's a slow process of sterilisation; even without the needles.
To care less and less, step by step until one believes one is happy.

IV

It's necessary now we have Automatic Number Plate Recognition
and A.T.O.S. Without it we wouldn't be able to keep the traffic flow
the paper trail; we wouldn't be able to see suffering people.

V

We wouldn't be able to see suffering people as inevitable
victims in a world that is selfish and unfair. We wouldn't be able
to swallow the story that says their stuff has nothing to do with us.

VI

It has no human cause. It isn't people who do that to people.
It's a divine bureaucracy we believe in more than God. A paper
construct that folds meaning into the municipality of misfortunes.

VII

It's the end product – the commodification of a lifetime
waiting for a train that never comes. The decaff from the new
vending machine is unspeakable, depressing; but on paper – one is fine.

None of the above

Stop beating yourself with this
club. Maybe folk who can't get
from one end of the day to the other
without drinking or drugs
really do see the world differently.

There was a knock at the door.
I answered it.
An old lady stood on the step.
She told me they had not received
my electoral registration form.

Hello I said.
She told me if I did not fill it in
I would lose My Right To Vote.
Can I help you? I said.

You will find It Difficult
To Obtain Credit, she read.
I'm sorry, I said. You're committing
a criminal offence and will be

fined One Thousand Pounds.
It's The Law, she said. I told her
it must be in the post.
I said that last year.

I don't want to lose
my democratic right to vote
for my dictator.
I closed the door.

in difference

*In memory of Angela Wrightson, who was murdered in her own
living room by two girls aged 13 and 14*

not giving a shit about the effects of decades of social and moral decay
is qualified by an inserted space
an interim   a breathing place a fag break or whatever
happened between the hours of 11pm and 2am on 8th December 2014
when Angela's attackers left her bloodied and battered on her living room
carpet
then returned to finish the job with a television set
an ad break   an intermission or the space
between the shutter being pressed and the image of Angela bruised and
terrified
uploaded on Snapchat Nah xx not that
kind of space but maybe your parking space
that your neighbour has taken up with his campervan marked auto sleeper
as though it were automatic going to sleep switching off
not giving a shit maybe I need more of it
sleep   space maybe I need to stop
joining dots filling blanks asking questions then I'll be able to nod off
automatically
just distance myself from the events of the day
as though it were as natural as breathing
shitting   pressing the space bar between words
so everything makes sense   everything is ordered words
are spelled this way not that way and have
commas and semi-colons   hyphens and spaces between them there are rules
about these things we all need to follow in order
to make the world a safe place for us to live in
together without beating each other to death however
different we are
from the neighbour with his campervan in your space
whom you believe is actually trying to make you feel inferior
smaller than average like Angela

who was five foot four and weighed six and a half stone
maybe this has nothing to do with space and is just a numbers game
like the national lottery like the fact that her killers were 13 and 14
had absconded from care 18 times in 30 days
before inflicting 70 slash wounds and 54 blunt force injuries on Angela's face
and body plus the 22 deflection injuries she sustained
including three fractured fingers as she tried to fend off blows during the six-hour attack
from as well as the television set a kettle
a coffee table a coal shovel a lump of wood and a computer printer
but that does not explain why they kicked her in the head
until pieces of her flesh flew off nor why they left
her naked with dirt smeared over her vagina
repeatedly over and over again
automatically as though it were an automatic thing
to blame the council people slipping
through the care system as though it were a net
full of holes dark spaces to fall into and get lost in
like the rules of grammar
repeatedly until it becomes an automatic thing
blow after blow again and again
because you are stupid and don't have a mind of your own
and need to be told
because you are stupid and you keep forgetting
that you are automatically stupid
and deserve to be beaten to death in your own living room
for being different for caring for sharing for giving
a shit you need to obey the rules
switch off and shut up shut down automatically
because Hartlepool Council Adult and Child Safeguarding Board
have commissioned two independent Serious Case Reviews
to determine whether any lessons can be learned
for people like Angela who have no voice police officer Steve Matthews says
he is not sure if it is a police or a social services problem
but authorities on Teesside say no
stone will be left unturned like it's an automatic thing

turning over stone after stone until the reason becomes apparent
why people posted threats on Facebook protesting
the death of one lost soul
by calling for the deaths of two more
Angela's mother says she will never forget
the images of her daughter's mutilated naked body
or the sight of Angela's living room where her blood was found
on all four walls the furniture the floor and the ceiling
she says if any positive can be taken
it is the kindness displayed by those who knew Angela best
after all what is a council if not a group of different people
who have forgotten what makes them the same
intoxicated by rules and regulations telling us where to go
for help where to sign our names who is to blame
what we have lost in the space between the decades
has nothing to do with governments or social services failures
and everything to do with how successful
they have been convincing us we are all
too stupid to be able to help ourselves.

Always read the label

These shirts were tested on animals.
They didn't fit
Into a large bowl
Made by really really pretty blonde girls
Inspired by deep fjords
Cocktails and a grandmother with exquisite taste

*

Mix all ingredients
Drag thru puddle behind car and blow dry on roof rack
Be nice to snails, hamsters and gerbils
The smaller you are
The more room there is
In your parents' basement

*

Don't be that guy
Always wash your butt
Tumble dry low
Remove promptly
And chill for several hours
Or if you lazy as shit get mama to do it

*

Do not wear for sumo wrestling
You can dance if you want to
No bleaching or shits gon
be fucked for real
You wouldn't understand
I have dental pain

*

Zip with caution
Contents may be hot
Please handle with as much love
As you would a 7-inch d***
Or give it to your mother
She knows how to do it

*

Nous sommes désolés que notre président est un idiot.
Nous n'avons pas voté pour lui.

Self-portrait with Onion

I bury my selves
under the chaff of seven separate veils
silence the texture of memory
in invisible ink

a brown-papered womb
I birth an heirloom
of recipes
a lifetime weeping and chopping

knife in hand   I strip
this shrink-wrapped ochre fist
of its skins and sickles
deliberate the innards of its dead weight

grief tastes no sweeter
peeled and scorched in a skillet
its signature dish
a scintilla

nestled beneath nibbled nailbed
feeds the aureole
of sadness
undressed

Gardening for Totalitarians

(For David Scott)

I have wondered at the watery impression
of Monet's paradise,
with its lily petals melting like lush brushstrokes,

promenaded the palatial paths and pavilions
of Versailles where the Sun King strolled,
been struck dumb by the virtuosity of Majorelle –

How its floral verdure harmonises cobalt
and ochre. Philosophers say the soul cannot
thrive in the absence of a garden. Just tiny tufts

of mustard and cress nestled in cardboard egg box cups,
a windowsill with parsley and coriander curled in pots
or a postage stamp of green out the back. Somewhere

inside everyone is a patch to tend. Perhaps that's why
the Scottish Government personified its state guardian scheme
by telling seven-year-olds to imagine

Scotland as a great garden, with each child
a plant growing in its soil. Where all the adults in their lives
were gardeners; except the State Named Person –

who was the Head Gardener. Who could fail
to find peace of mind cultivating our common seed?
Picture the patchwork landscape of family life dug up

calculate the yield. When mother and father
are humbled *tattie howkers* in their own homes
what will become of the weeds?

The presence of solitude

One night, waiting for sleep
another came to rest beside,
another grown old and tired
of clocks and days and numbers.

I did not hear her soft step
or feel her slip beneath sheets
like a sleepless child.
Motionless, we lie together

listening to the faint rattle
of a far-away train
a vixen's shriek, a drunk
in the street stumbling through

'Singing in the Rain'. Immersed
in the inverse jurisdiction
of midnight and artificial light,
we watch the moon untangle her hair

before she floats away
to find the next dressing table mirror
to gloat in. I cannot see
my companion's face

though I imagine her pale,
silver-fox fair. Outside, I catch
the slap of morning tide
against fishing boat's side

the spat of raindrops breaking on glass.
I turn to take her in my arms.
as morning cracks
and the sky begins its pouring.

Thursday Afternoon at the Supermarket

Somewhere between the lunchtime rush and
the afterwork crush, in the never-never
measure of foil-wrapped wonder I forgot
there was no room in my fridge for twenty-
four tubs of yoghurt on BOGOF and filled
my gondola, before floating off into another
aisle with teenage mums mouthing the lyrics
to *muzak* and toddlers arcing out of trolleys
and rows and rows of powdered milk and
pastel coloured plastic bottles perched on
shelves. My hand reached for the swell of
my belly. As, in a clash of strip-lights and
metallic hums and no-frills special offers
succumbed, I fell into the aisle of years long
gone. I forgot the dreadful flush of my
empty stomach, the last part of myself,
carried away.

Portrait of the Self as All Day Breakfast

The self is an unremarkable number.
Its feet an institution – tasteless bulk-

buys, deep-fried, cremated. Its legs
two fat sausages – stumped, fatigued.

Forked with resentment they lard
the lean earth. Its baked-bean belly –

a bodge-job – fills the *manyana*
like expanding foam – restraining

empty slicks with Daddie's Sauce. Its heart
a tomato – severed, scorched aborted –

floats on a raft of stale bread – soaking
the leftovers of ritual sacrifice – tongue

thick-sliced, discharged. Its breasts
suns once – now gobs of yolk and stuffing.

Its thoughts form lingering crusts
of grease and shame and nothing.

Ghazal for Carys

Without her, roped in the nothingness
between being and becoming – I am nothing.

I am tied inside the mirror, splintered tongues
tracing my skin in thin red lines – Really, it's nothing.

I am drawn into a one-colour drone
where the argot of semi-tones is nothing.

Without her, a part of the world departs the world
like wetness leaving water leaving nothing.

Her lips mark a crossing where alone will never find us
where parting is choice, where pain is nothing.

Her thread undoes the other-half of my heart
stirs the you in me where once was nothing.

In Memory of Effie May Leah, 1922-2016

And she is everywhere
Reminding us we are all stardust
Life's a game, spades and hearts, you said
The endless food of love *ad libitum*
In our conversations outside the crematorium
Like we'd been taken somewhere magical
As Nick Drake sang 'From The Morning'
Your breath returning to the wind
You walked with *The Women*
For Life on Earth
All the way from west Wales to Greenham Common
A campsite, hash cookies, tarot cards racing through your mind
Ten years with no electricity and no running
Water
Where the restless river finds the still body of
A butterfly who loved a mole
Then scratched a living from seven acres of windswept moorland
For a woman who knew a life of servants
A cardboard coffin bought in the summer of '76
Held together with parcel tape, dressed in Holly and Ivy
No tax, no MOT and two fingers to the funeral directors
In Howie's rusty red Renault Trafic
You followed your own road
The endless coloured ways

The endless coloured ways
You followed your own road
In Howie's rusty red Renault Trafic
No tax, no MOT and two fingers to the funeral directors
Held together with parcel tape, dressed in Holly and Ivy
A cardboard coffin bought in the summer of '76
For a woman who knew a life of servants
Then scratched a living from seven acres of windswept moorland
A butterfly who loved a mole

Where the restless river finds the still body of
Water
Ten years with no electricity and no running
A campsite, hash cookies, tarot cards racing through your mind
All the way from west Wales to Greenham Common
For life on earth
You walked with the women
Your breath returning to the wind
As Nick Drake sang 'From The Morning'
Like we'd been taken somewhere magical
In our conversations outside the crematorium
The endless food of love ad-libitum
Life's a game of spades and hearts, you said
Reminding us we are all stardust
And she is everywhere

Double Figures

Down the Netpool Fields
before they built the new playground

you tiptoed over the monkey bars
like a tom cat.

I haloed your loose limbs
as the wind scissored

your ruby fringe
and the older kids

who hung out there stopped
swigging Special Brew looked up

and cheered your light years.
You were halfway across

and the seconds swayed like hours
when you paused

and bowed to your audience
of under-fives and underage drinkers

so fluently
I mistook your smile for the sunset.

When you reached the other side
the street lights whispered time

then blushed in admiration.
You called out to me   waving –

your silhouette   bold
against bare branches

my heart poised
as a leaf before it falls.

moon in scorpio

sour days under stone-dead sun
ghosts of children in the park
arcing the swing, vanishing
only voices left to whisper
lost, lost, lost

in a frozen
acoustic, autumn leaves
bring their final, bloodless
blaze, even birdsong bitters the sky
with the sting of the long walk home

Last Impression

who could sit in your chair
the only thing left
bearing any true likeness of yourself

smelling of Navy Cut
and old rope
wearing the impact of chronic depression

what good are photographs
doorways to death
they capture only the presence of yourself

outside the first snow of evening falls
covering the imprint of loss
with another layer of memory

I will not disturb
the sagging seat pad
of its dusty slumbering sway

how else will we tell
other than through this soft scoop,
this last impression of your inner life

How silent is it?

it was my house
but I was not
my eye

where do I hang

my coat
my keys
my memories ... ?

Portion

after W. G. Sebald

count chickens
& remember the horizon
has already eaten the dust

break bread
then build walls & ceiling
from crumbs & crusts

cover the hollow
splendid hall
mark your presence with an X

swallow salt
as a sign of loss
do not look back

Notes

'Five Spot Blues' is an instrumental piece.

The Stuffed Walrus has been on display at the Horniman Museum in south London for more than a century. It is an unusual taxidermy specimen; appearing stretched and 'over stuffed'. It lacks the skin folds characteristic of a walrus in the wild because, over one hundred years ago, only a few people had ever seen a live walrus. It remains one of the most popular exhibits in the museum.

The epigram for 'Postcard from *Pwll Deri*' is carved into a rock above this popular viewpoint on the Pembrokeshire Coastal Path.

The phrase 'O for my dead body' is from the cockney alphabet.

'traffic' engages with an ode by Joseph Straus, the class poet at Ohio University Class of 1891 and chief engineer of the Golden Gate Bridge. Straus wrote the lines to mark the occasion of the bridge's opening, where he remarked to reporters, 'Who would want to jump from the Golden Gate Bridge?'

All the events described in 'The art of moving an upright piano into an upstairs flat' are true.

The lines *'The endless coloured ways'* and *'And she is everywhere'* are lyrics from Nick Drake's 'From The Morning' from the album *Pink Moon* (Island, 1972). *The women for Life on Earth* is the name of the women's collective who walked from west Wales to Berkshire and established the anti-nuclear peace camp at RAF Greenham Common in 1981. Effie's memorial was conducted without assistance from funeral directors; her body being transported to the crematorium in a cardboard coffin in the back of her son's van.

The lines comprising 'Always read the label' were all found on garment care labels.

'On paper' was inspired by the poetry of Martin Glaz Serup.

Tattie howkers were seasonal migrant potato diggers, who came over from Ireland to harvest the potato crop throughout Scotland from the nineteenth century until the late 1980's. In 2014 the Scottish Parliament passed legislation to appoint a 'Named Person' or state official tasked with looking after every child's 'wellbeing' and 'happiness' – terms which are not defined in law. The data-sharing provisions on which the scheme relies have been declared illegal by the UK Supreme Court, with one judge commenting, 'The first thing that a totalitarian regime tries to do is to get to the children, to distance them from the subversive, varied influences of their families and indoctrinate them in their rulers' view of the world.'

Acknowledgements

With thanks to the editors of the following publications in which some of these poems, or earlier versions of them, first appeared or are due to appear: *Poetry Wales, New Welsh Review, Brittle Star, I am not a silent poet, NRW Digital, Obsessed With Pipework, Orbis, Sentinel Literary Quarterly, The Lampeter Review, The North, Under the Radar.*

A selection of these poems formed the pamphlet *moon in scorpio* which was shortlisted for The Venture Award 2015.

'Unspoken II' was highly commended in the Penfro Book Festival Poetry Competitions 2015, 2016.

'The Magician's Daughter' and 'Romeo y Julieta' were highly commended in The Camden and Lumen Poetry Competition 2016.

'A river runs through me,' won the *Orbis* issue#198 Reader's Award.

'The art of moving an upright piano into an upstairs flat' was highly commended in the Welsh International Poetry Competition 2017.

'On the morning of September 11, 2001' was runner-up in The Cellar Bards Poetry Slam 2017.

Special thanks to Samantha Wynne-Rhydderch and Literature Wales for generous support with writing and assembling the collection, and Helen May Williams for help in preparing the manuscript.

PARTHIAN *Poetry in Translation*

Home on the Move
Two poems go on a journey
Edited by Manuela Perteghella
and Ricarda Vidal
ISBN 978-1-912681-46-4
£8.99 | Paperback
'One of the most inventive and necessary
poetry projects of recent years...'
– Chris McCabe

Pomegranate Garden
A selection of poems by Haydar Ergülen
Edited by Mel Kenne, Saliha Paker
and Caroline Stockford
ISBN 978-1-912681-42-6
£8.99 | Paperback
'A major poet who rises from [his] roots to touch
on what is human at its most stripped-down,
vulnerable and universal...'
– Michel Cassir, *L'Harmattan*

Modern Bengali Poetry
Arunava Sinha
ISBN 978-1-912681-22-8
£11.99 | Paperback
This volume celebrates over one hundred years
of poetry from the two Bengals represented
by over fifty different poets.

PARTHIAN *Poetry*

Hey Bert
Roberto Pastore
ISBN 978-1-912109-34-0
£9.00 | Paperback
'Bert's writing, quite simply, makes me happy.
Jealous but happy.'
– **Crystal Jeans**

Sliced Tongue and Pearl Cufflinks
Kittie Belltree
ISBN 978-1-912681-14-3
£9.00 | Paperback
'By turns witty and sophisticated, her writing shivers
with a suggestion of unease that is compelling.'
– **Samantha Wynne-Rhydderch**

Hymns Ancient & Modern
New & Selected Poems
J. Brookes
ISBN 978-1-912681-33-4
£9.99 | Paperback
'It's a skilful writer indeed who can combine elements both
heartbreaking and hilarious: Brookes is that writer.'
– **Robert Minhinnick**

The Filthy Quiet
Kate Noakes
ISBN 978-1-91-268102-0
£8.99 | Paperback
'Kate Noakes' *The Filthy Quiet* is ... always
brightly striking onwards, generating
its own irresistible energy.'
– **Jane Commane**